sacristy prayers

for every sunday of the lectionary

Nick Fawcett

kevin mayhew

First published in 2005 by

KEVIN MAYHEW LTD
Buxhall, Stowmarket, Suffolk, IP14 3BW
E-mail: info@kevinmayhewltd.com

9 8 7 6 5 4 3 2 1 0

ISBN 1 84417 369 0
Catalogue No 1500773

Cover design by Angela Selfe
Edited and typeset by Katherine Laidler

Printed in Great Britain

Contents

8

Acknowledgements

I have been enormously helped in the writing of this book by Father Philip Shryane, parish priest of Bury St Edmunds, Suffolk, not only for his guidance but also for his careful editing of the original manuscript. As well as suggesting numerous revisions, he at times suggested entirely new wordings that I was able to build upon. I am extremely grateful for his invaluable assistance.

Introduction

It's Sunday, and there are just a few minutes to go before the start of Mass: time for a brief prayer with the servers. But what words to use? You may prefer to use your own, or perhaps have a stock of tried and trusted prayers for every occasion, but at times you may feel the need for a fresh approach, an alternative wording that offers a different perspective.

This book is written with that in mind. Covering the three-year cycle of the Lectionary, with additional material for special feasts days, the prayers are written in everyday language and linked to the Gospel reading or occasion in question. The aim is to offer a brief introduction to the theme for the day, focusing minds upon God, and consecrating to him both the act of worship and the worshippers themselves. If it helps to achieve that goal it will have been well worth the writing.

NICK FAWCETT

YEAR A

Nov 2010 — Nov 2011

First Sunday of Advent

Lord Jesus Christ,
    draw near to us in this Advent season,
    and stir our hearts at the message of your coming
    and coming again.
Help us to recognise your presence among us,
    in our work, our lives and our world,
    and in serving you now
    may we be ready to welcome you always
    as King of kings and Lord of lords.
Amen.

Second Sunday of Advent

God of all,
    as you prepared the way of the Lord through your servant John,
    making hearts and minds ready to receive him,
    so prepare us now to respond in turn,
    welcoming him gladly and freely into our lives,
    and devoting ourselves to your service
    in his name.
Amen.

Third Sunday of Advent

Gracious God,
    as you spoke through John the Baptist,
    and through the prophets before him,
    speak to us now through this time of worship.
Open our ears, minds and souls to your word of truth,
    the Word made flesh,
    Jesus Christ our Lord.
Amen.

Fourth Sunday of Advent

Lord Jesus Christ,
   born of Mary,
   coming to our world through her,
   be born afresh in us
   that we might be born again through you.
Draw close to us now,
   and open our hearts
   so that we may reach out to the world,
   bringing hope and healing,
   to the glory of your name.
Amen.

Christmas Day

Loving God,
   though we have heard the Christmas message so many times before,
   speak through it again today,
   granting us new insights and deeper understanding
   so that our faith in the mystery of the word made flesh
   may be enriched
   and our joy increase.
Reveal your Son to us once more,
   good news for all people
   yesterday, today and for ever,
   Jesus Christ, our Lord.
Amen.

The Holy Family

Loving God,
   as we celebrate your entering our world as a baby,
   lovingly nurtured through childhood by Mary and Joseph,
   open our hearts today to the richness of family life,
   and to everything it offers in so many ways.
Inspire and equip us in turn
   to do all we can in building up our own family life,
   in his name.
Amen.

Second Sunday of Christmas

Lord Jesus Christ,
   we come to you in worship,
   rejoicing that you made your home among us,
   sharing our life and death in order to bring us new birth,
   forgiveness
   and a fresh start.
Come again now, we ask,
   and through your grace work within us,
   cleansing us of all that is wrong in our lives and unworthy of your love.
Draw us closer to you each day
   and lead us in the way of truth,
   so that, growing in faith,
   we might know and do your will,
   to the glory of God the Father.
Amen.

The Epiphany of the Lord

Living God,
   as you led wise men to your Son,
   reveal him also to us;
   as you guided them on their journey,
   guide us as we travel through life;
   as you spoke *to* and *through* them,
   do likewise with us;
   and as they responded in joyful worship,
   so may we in turn,
   to the glory of his name.
Amen.

The Baptism of the Lord

Redeemer Christ,
   we remember today your baptism in the Jordan,
   a defining moment at the start of your ministry.
Challenge us through your teaching and service
   to consider our own faith and response,
   and to commit ourselves again to the growth of your kingdom.
Amen.

Ash Wednesday

Heavenly Father,
   we come at the start of this season of Lent,
   conscious of our weakness and sin,
   but aware also that you are a God of mercy and compassion.
Renew us, we pray, through our prayer, fasting and service,
   so that, through this time, we might renew our commitment
   and walk the way of Christ with greater faith and confidence.
Amen.

First Sunday of Lent

Search us, O God, and know our thoughts.
Examine us, and reveal our faults.
Cleanse us, and make us new.
Touch us, and make us whole.
Receive our worship and hear our prayer,
   in Jesus' name.
Amen.

Second Sunday of Lent

God of love,
   we come in faith,
   trusting in your word
   and rejoicing in your gift of life.
Teach us, as we worship,
   to spend more time alone with you in prayer,
   so that, here and everywhere,
   we may glimpse your glory
   and joyfully respond,
   through Jesus Christ our Lord.
Amen.

Third Sunday of Lent

God of Spirit and truth,
    we thirst to know you better,
    to grow closer to you each day.
Reach out now,
    and pour out your grace upon us,
    so that your love may well up in our hearts,
    and living water flow deep within,
    through Jesus Christ our Lord.
Amen.

Fourth Sunday of Lent

Gracious God,
    open our eyes to your goodness, love and mercy,
    for so often we fail to see as clearly as we should,
    our minds closed to what we would rather not face.
Give us now, as we worship you,
    deeper insight into who and what you are
    and a clearer picture of all you would do among us.
In Christ's name we pray.
Amen.

Fifth Sunday of Lent

Living God,
    for the way you turn sorrow to joy,
    doubt to faith,
    despair to hope,
    and death to life,
    we praise you.
Put your hand upon us,
    and through this time set apart for you
    continue to make us new.
Take what we are,
    and, by the power of your resurrection,
    shape what we shall be,
    through Jesus Christ our Lord.
Amen.

Palm Sunday

Lord Jesus Christ,
    we come to declare your greatness,
    to acclaim you as king,
    and to seek your will for our lives.
Through this celebration teach us the true meaning of power
    and the nature of your kingdom,
    so that we may commit ourselves more fully to you
    and gain a clearer understanding of your purpose for all.
Amen.

Maundy Thursday

Lord Jesus Christ,
    remembering how, at the Last Supper,
    you shared bread and wine with your disciples –
    your body broken,
    your blood poured out,
    given in humble service –
    so we come now, at your generous invitation,
    to eat and drink in turn.
At this table of word and sacrifice,
    help us, through all we share and celebrate,
    to enter generously into service of you and others,
    to your glory.
Amen.

Good Friday

Lord Jesus Christ,
    help us to follow you on the journey to Calvary,
    retracing your footsteps with love and thanksgiving.
Remind us how, through the cross,
    you have won for us forgiveness,
    enduring the darkness of sorrow, suffering and death
    to win us life.
Lord Jesus, we thank you.
Amen.

Easter Day

Mighty God,
  we rejoice today at the resurrection of Jesus,
  his triumph over hatred, evil and death,
  and, in awe and wonder,
  we thank you for calling us to share in his victory,
  celebrating life now and for all eternity.
Help us to bring the joy and hope of this good news
  to all we meet.
Amen.

Second Sunday of Easter

Lord Jesus Christ,
  we remember how you came to your disciples,
  breaking into their sorrow, confusion and fear,
  speaking your word of peace.
May that Easter gift grow in our hearts and our world each day,
  dispelling the clouds of doubt and disbelief,
  and bringing the inner peace and stillness
  that you alone can give.
Amen.

Third Sunday of Easter

Lord Jesus Christ,
  as those who walked with you on the road to Emmaus
  recognised you in the breaking of bread,
  so may we recognise you now as we celebrate Mass.
Open our hearts today to your living presence,
  that our hearts may burn within us
  as we strive to walk in your way.
Amen.

Fourth Sunday of Easter

Lord Jesus Christ,
    shepherd of the sheep,
    help us once more today to hear your voice
    and to follow you.
Call us back when we go astray,
    and show us again the right path,
    the way leading to true and abundant life,
    now and for all eternity.
Amen.

Fifth Sunday of Easter

Lord Jesus Christ,
    we believe you to be the way, the truth and the life.
Guide us now, as we celebrate this Mass,
    so that we may walk with you more closely,
    believe in you more deeply
    and live for you more fully,
    to the glory of God the Father.
Amen.

Sixth Sunday of Easter

Loving God,
    help us to worship you,
    through faithful discipleship and obedience to your will.
Draw near through your Spirit of truth,
    and, through the power of the risen Christ,
    transform our lives and make us new,
    so that we may praise you now and always,
    to the greater glory of your name.
Amen.

The Ascension of the Lord

Lord Jesus Christ,
    ascended yet with us always,
    at the right hand of the Father yet interceding there on our behalf,
    teach us today what it means to serve you,
    how best we can work for your kingdom,
    not just in words but also in deeds,
    not just at Mass but in the reality of our lives.
In your name we ask it.
Amen.

Seventh Sunday of Easter

Holy Father,
    help us to be true to your name
    as we listen to your word
    and to receive your Son, Jesus, in Holy Communion.
Teach us your will:
    to recognise that, above all, you long for us to be one –
    with Christ,
    with you,
    and with your people everywhere –
    united in love,
    and striving together for the growth of your kingdom
    and the fulfilment of your purpose.
Live in us, that we might live for you,
    this day and always.
Amen.

Pentecost

Spirit of God,
   come among us,
   move among us,
   work among us.
Breathe life into our worship,
   love into our hearts
   and light into our witness.
Come as fire,
   refining and cleansing.
Come as wind,
   blowing the cobwebs from our lives.
Come as a dove,
   enfolding us in your peace.
Come *to* us,
   move *in* us,
   work *through* us,
   now and always.
Amen.

Trinity Sunday

God our Father,
   your ways are not our ways,
   nor your thoughts our thoughts,
   but you reach out and welcome us in love.
God the Son,
   our lives are troubled,
   weighed down by heavy burdens.
   until we rest in you.
God the Spirit,
   enrich our faith,
   and enfold us in your love,
   so that, knowing you more fully,
   we may serve you more faithfully.
Holy Trinity,
   draw us into your love and unity.
Amen.

Second Sunday in Ordinary Time

Father God,
  help us, like John the Baptist before us
  and so many others who have followed in his footsteps,
  to see the light of Christ and bear witness to it.
Open our lives, through your Spirit, to his presence among us now,
  and help us to live in such a way that his light may shine *in* us,
  and *through* us,
  bringing glory to you.
Amen.

Third Sunday in Ordinary Time

God our Father,
  without your light in our lives we walk in darkness,
  denied the joy, hope and guidance that you alone can give.
May that light break more fully into our hearts through Christ,
  so that, like his first disciples, we may follow his way with joy,
  and bring light to others in turn.
Amen.

Fourth Sunday in Ordinary Time

Lord Jesus Christ,
  as you taught the crowds on the mountaintop,
  so now teach us as we gather in your name.
Prompt us through your Spirit,
  that we may hear and understand your word,
  and put it into action in all we do and are,
  to your glory.
Amen.

Fifth Sunday in Ordinary Time

Lord Jesus Christ,
   shine in our hearts and work within us,
   so that, as your people,
   through your grace,
   we may honour your call to be salt of the earth
   and light of the world,
   to the praise of our Father in heaven.
Amen.

Sixth Sunday in Ordinary Time

Lord Jesus,
   remembering that you came to fulfil the law and the prophets,
   teach us, we pray, to act justly,
   love tenderly
   and walk humbly in your way,
   honouring *their* message
   and *your* will.
Amen.

Seventh Sunday in Ordinary Time

God our Father,
   as we strive to love you more each day
   teach us what that means in practice.
Help us, each day, to face up to the challenge it entails –
   praying for our enemies
   and giving without counting the cost.
So, by your grace, may we learn to love others
   as fully as you love us,
   through Jesus Christ our Lord.
Amen.

Eighth Sunday in Ordinary Time

Heavenly Father,
   help us to recognise your presence
   in the wonder and beauty of creation,
   seeing all around us signs of your love
   and evidence of your care.
So may we trust ever more deeply in your grace,
   goodness and faithfulness,
   through Jesus Christ our Lord.
Amen.

Ninth Sunday in Ordinary Time

Living God,
   help us today, as we hear your word, to act upon it,
   consecrating our lives to you
   and committing ourselves again to your service.
Awaken us to all you would say,
   and teach us to build our lives upon Christ,
   our faith founded in him so that it is able to withstand
   whatever storms life may throw at it.
Speak now,
   and give us ears to hear,
   in his name.
Amen.

Tenth Sunday in Ordinary Time

Lord Jesus Christ,
   we remember how you saw in Matthew a true follower,
   calling him to be both a disciple and a writer of the Gospel.
We celebrate that you invite us also to follow,
   seeing someone of value beneath outward appearances,
   and calling us to turn from our sins and walk in your way.
Help us to live the gospel truthfully and with a generous heart.
Amen.

Eleventh Sunday in Ordinary Time

Lord Jesus Christ,
   we come to you,
   the source of life and bringer of peace.
As your disciples today,
   help us to reach out in your name,
   carrying the good news to a bruised and broken world,
   and showing through our life and witness your care for all.
Amen.

Twelfth Sunday in Ordinary Time

Heavenly Father,
   for the knowledge that we can come before you
   assured always of a welcome,
   confident of your love and care,
   we praise you.
Teach us to value you as much as you value us,
   through Jesus Christ our Lord.
Amen.

Thirteenth Sunday in Ordinary Time

Lord Jesus Christ,
   give us the courage we need to pick up our cross,
   and to bear both the privilege yet burden of living the gospel.
Work *in* us and *through* us,
   that others may recognise through our lives
   your message of love and welcome.
Amen.

Fourteenth Sunday in Ordinary Time

Lord Jesus Christ,
   you invite all who are weary of carrying heavy burdens
   to find help and strength in you,
   and so we come now,
   seeking to let go of all the problems and worries
   that weigh us down.
Help us to learn of you,
   and in your way of humility and gentleness
   to find rest for our souls.
Amen.

Fifteenth Sunday in Ordinary Time

Living God,
   as we meet together now,
   sow the seed of your word in our hearts.
May it find a place to grow,
   despite all that competes for space and time in our lives.
May shoots of faith be able to withstand
   the temptations and pressures that threaten to choke them.
May new growth be seen among us,
   leading to a rich harvest of lives won for you.
In Christ's name we ask it.
Amen.

Sixteenth Sunday in Ordinary Time

God of justice and truth, yet also of love and mercy,
   focus our thoughts upon you
   so that we may be open to fresh insights into truth,
   new horizons in faith
   and a deeper understanding of your purpose.
Help us to stand up against evil
   and to work together for good,
   recognising that you long to redeem us all
   and will not willingly lose anyone.
Amen.

Seventeenth Sunday in Ordinary Time

God of all,
   open our hearts and minds to your presence among us,
   and to your work in our lives and our world.
Help us never to lose sight of the treasure of your kingdom,
   but to recognise the way it is growing around us.
Teach us, then, to commit ourselves wholeheartedly to Christ
   by doing whatever we can to bring its fulfilment closer.
Amen.

Eighteenth Sunday in Ordinary Time

Heavenly Father,
   we bring you our spiritual hunger,
   our yearning for inner peace,
   knowing that you alone can feed our souls,
   and do so in ways beyond all our expectations.
Reach out to all gathered here today,
   filling us with spiritual food –
   bread of life and living water –
   so that our faith may be nourished
   and commitment strengthened,
   through Jesus Christ our Lord.
Amen.

Nineteenth Sunday in Ordinary Time

Lord Jesus Christ,
   speak your word now in the turmoil of our world,
   in the confusion of life,
   and especially in the hearts of those present today
   who are disturbed by sorrow and distress.
Bring order out of chaos,
   confidence out of fear,
   faith out of doubt
   and peace out of unrest,
   giving us the certain knowledge that nothing,
   not even death itself,
   can finally overwhelm us.
In your name we pray.
Amen.

Twentieth Sunday in Ordinary Time

Gracious God,
    help us to see not the outside but the person beneath;
    to look beyond appearances to the thoughts of the heart.
Save us, then, from empty show or superficial piety,
    and teach us to approach you instead in faith and humility,
    knowing that your love extends to all who truly seek you,
    through Jesus Christ our Lord.
Amen.

Twenty-first Sunday in Ordinary Time

Loving Lord,
    once more we confess our faith in you,
    acknowledging you as the Messiah,
    the Son of the living God,
    the one who sets us free and brings us life.
Help us to honour you
    not only in words but also through living faithfully as your people,
    your Body,
    your Church,
    working for and witnessing to your kingdom in word and deed.
Amen.

Twenty-second Sunday in Ordinary Time

Lord Jesus Christ,
    we want to honour you by living as your disciples
    and walking in your way,
    but we find it hard
    because our inclinations are so very different to your own.
Reveal to us, we pray, more of what it means to follow you,
    more about being a true disciple.
Help us to grasp the meaning of your kingdom,
    where losers are winners,
    the first are last
    and those who lose their life for your sake will truly find it.
Teach us now,
    by your grace.
Amen.

Twenty-third Sunday in Ordinary Time

Lord Jesus Christ,
    you promise that where two or three are gathered in your name,
    you will be there in the midst of them,
    and so we come now,
    eager to meet with you:
    to hear your voice,
    receive your guidance,
    offer our worship
    and do your will.
Come among us through your Spirit
    and help us to sense your nearness.
Fill our hearts and minds,
    so that when we return to the daily business of life
    we will know you with us there too
    and be equipped to walk in your way,
    faithful and true to our journey's end.
Amen.

Twenty-fourth Sunday in Ordinary Time

God our Father,
    speak to us through your willingness to forgive and go on forgiving,
    and help us to forgive in turn,
    striving to heal broken relationships,
    mend quarrels,
    and start afresh.
Teach us through the example of Christ
    to show something of the mercy you have shown to us.
Amen.

Twenty-fifth Sunday in Ordinary Time

Loving Father,
    help us today to grasp the extent of your love,
    the breadth of your purpose
    and the scope of your grace –
    to recognise that no one is beyond your mercy
    or outside your concern.
Teach us to be generous in our dealings with others,
    as you have so generously dealt with us,
    through Jesus Christ our Lord.
Amen.

Twenty-sixth Sunday in Ordinary Time

Lord Jesus Christ,
    teach us to recognise your authority in our lives
    and to respond freely to your call.
Show us what you would have us do
    and how you want us to serve you.
Help us each day to recognise our need of you
    and to receive again the love and pardon you delight to give.
Amen.

Twenty-seventh Sunday in Ordinary Time

Loving God,
    help us to recognise where we fail you,
    where our commitment is weak,
    and the harvest poor.
Come to us afresh,
    bringing growth in grace,
    that we may bear fruit for you,
    our life and witness reflecting your love,
    through Jesus Christ our Lord.
Amen.

Twenty-eighth Sunday in Ordinary Time

Living God,
   as we celebrate and eat at your table,
   prepare our hearts and minds to receive all you offer.
Fill us with your gifts of love, joy, peace,
   goodness, compassion and humility –
   that we may freely offer ourselves in the service of Christ,
   who lives and reigns, now and for ever.
Amen.

Twenty-ninth Sunday in Ordinary Time

Lord of all,
   teach us as citizens of heaven to live as citizens of earth,
   and thus to honour you.
Show us what it means to be your people in the daily business of life;
   how best to fulfil our responsibilities and duties to others
   while staying true to you.
Give us wisdom and faith to walk as your people,
   in your world,
   to your glory.
Amen.

Thirtieth Sunday in Ordinary Time

Almighty God,
   touch our lives through your Spirit,
   and renew us through the grace of Christ,
   that we may better keep your commandments.
Help us truly to love you with heart, mind and soul,
   and to love our neighbour as ourselves.
Amen.

Thirty-first Sunday in Ordinary Time

Eternal God,
    lead our thoughts today
    and our lives always,
    strengthening us in times of testing
    and protecting us from evil.
Give us strength to follow you through joy or sorrow,
    trusting in your saving love,
    through Jesus Christ our Lord.
Amen.

Thirty-second Sunday in Ordinary Time

Lord Jesus Christ,
    prepare our hearts to meet you
    both in this time of worship,
    and when you return in glory to establish your kingdom.
Fill us with your Spirit,
    so that we will be awake and ready to welcome you
    when you call us.
Amen.

Thirty-third Sunday in Ordinary Time

Lord Jesus Christ,
    teach us to live faithfully for you,
    using the gifts you have given us in your service.
Help us to worship you in all we do,
    consecrating our lives to building up your kingdom,
    for you live and reign for evermore.
Amen.

Christ the King

Lord Jesus Christ,
    awaken us to your presence around us,
    especially in the cry of the needy,
    and in responding to the hungry, sick,
    lonely and oppressed,
    may we know that we are serving you,
    our Lord and King.
Amen.

YEAR B

First Sunday of Advent

Lord Jesus Christ,
    teach us that, just as you walked this earth,
    sharing our humanity even to death,
    so you are here now through your Spirit,
    eager to show your love and grace.
Grant, then, as we come together in your name,
    that we might know your presence,
    hear your voice
    and receive your blessing.
Amen.

Second Sunday of Advent

Faithful God,
    as we prepare to celebrate the birth of your Son,
    speak to us through your word
    and touch our lives afresh.
Break down all that separates us from you,
    all that obscures your love
    and frustrates your purpose.
Pour out your Spirit,
    that we may be ready to serve you,
    in his name.
Amen.

Third Sunday of Advent

God our Father,
    through the words of Isaiah and John the Baptist
    we are reminded today of the challenge of the gospel.
Speak through their testimony,
    and help us each day to follow Jesus,
    the one to whom they point,
    responding with a generous heart
    in grateful praise and joyful service.
Amen.

Fourth Sunday of Advent

Almighty God,
  we celebrate today how you chose to use Mary to fulfil your purpose,
  and how, humbly and wholeheartedly, she responded.
Help us, as we hear your word,
  to respond with similar obedience,
  prepared to be used as you see fit.
Amen.

Christmas Day

God of love,
  as the shepherds hurried to Bethlehem,
  eager to see your Son for themselves,
  so we come now,
  to rejoice in Christ's presence
  and to offer him our worship.
Direct our thoughts and actions
  that we may see more fully the wonder of this season
  and the good news it proclaims for all people.
Amen.

The Holy Family

Father of all,
  we remember today how your Son came among us within a family,
  growing and becoming strong in spirit within his childhood home.
Be present, we ask, in our homes and family life today,
  helping us to recognise him in those close to us
  and to reveal him in turn,
  his light shining through everything we do and say.
Amen.

Second Sunday of Christmas

Creator God,
    made known to us in the Word made flesh,
    revealing your grace and truth through him
    and bringing light into the darkness of our world,
    come again to us now
    and dwell among us through your Spirit.
Breathe your life into us,
    so that your Word might speak to our hearts
    and shine from our lives,
    to your glory.
Amen.

The Epiphany of the Lord

Lord Jesus Christ,
    hope of your people,
    hope of your world,
    touch our lives as we gather before you.
Shine in our hearts
    and light up our minds,
    so that we will grasp more clearly
    the hope you give us
    and the joy of life in all its fullness.
Amen.

The Baptism of the Lord

Lord Jesus Christ,
    we praise you today for your obedience to God's call,
    embracing the way of service and suffering,
    so that we might become children of God.
Give us a clearer understanding of all that means,
    so that we may commit ourselves more fully to you.
Amen.

Ash Wednesday

Eternal Father,
    as we worship you today and throughout this season of Lent,
    help us to recognise all that is wrong in our lives,
    all that separates us from you and others.
Help us, prayerfully and humbly, to examine ourselves
    and to acknowledge our faults,
    so that we may receive healing and forgiveness,
    through Jesus Christ our Lord.
Amen.

First Sunday of Lent

Lord Jesus Christ,
    as you wrestled in the wilderness with temptation,
    with the nature of your calling,
    help us today,
    and throughout this time of Lent,
    to hear your voice
    and to understand what you ask of us.
Fix our thoughts on you
    and direct all that we do,
    so that we may grow in grace
    and stand firm in faith.
Amen.

Second Sunday of Lent

Lord Jesus Christ,
    it is good for us to be here,
    good to honour your glory.
Help us through glimpsing you more fully
    to offer ourselves afresh in your service,
    taking up our cross
    and walking where you lead us.
Amen.

Third Sunday of Lent

Lord Jesus Christ,
    as you cleansed the temple in Jerusalem,
    so come now to our lives and cleanse our hearts,
    removing all that destroys our relationship with you.
Re-create us,
    making our bodies into a living temple of your Holy Spirit,
    through your redeeming and renewing love.
Amen.

Fourth Sunday of Lent

Loving Father,
    you remind us today of how much you love us
    and how much you do for us.
Help us to respond by consecrating our lives to Christ,
    so that his grace may flow into our hearts,
    leading us out of darkness into his marvellous light.
Amen.

Fifth Sunday of Lent

Lord Jesus Christ,
    speak to us of the new life you have made possible
    through your sacrifice on the cross.
Unfold to us the true nature of discipleship –
    what it means to love and follow you –
    and help us, by your grace, to respond,
    dying to self
    and rising to new life with you,
    so that all we do and are may be offered in your service
    and to your glory.
Amen.

Palm Sunday

Lord Jesus Christ,
  we greet and acclaim you,
    remembering how crowds joyfully welcomed you into Jerusalem,
    but remembering also how a mob bayed there for your death.
Strengthen and nurture our faith,
    that the commitment we profess today may be as real tomorrow,
    and every day,
    as it is now,
    to the glory of your name.
Amen.

Maundy Thursday

Lord Jesus Christ,
  we remember today your humility,
    your kneeling to wash the disciples' feet.
We remember your love as you broke bread and shared wine,
    offering your body and blood to bring life to the world.
Fill us now with your grace as we share the Eucharist together,
    that lovingly and humbly we may serve one another in turn,
    to the glory of your name.
Amen.

Good Friday

Lord Jesus Christ,
  like those who stood at the foot of the cross,
    as you breathed your last,
    help us today to glimpse the wonder of your love,
    and the awful reality of what you suffered.
Help us to understand how much you love us,
    and how much you were ready to sacrifice
    to overcome everything that keeps us from you,
    and may that knowledge feed our faith
    and deepen our discipleship.
Amen.

Easter Day

Lord Jesus Christ,
    as Mary recognised you in the garden,
    as disciples met you on the Emmaus Road,
    as the Apostles encountered you standing among them,
    may we meet you now,
    our Risen Lord and Saviour,
    conqueror of evil,
    triumphant over death.
On this Easter day, we acknowledge your greatness,
    and celebrate the new life you have given.
Amen.

Second Sunday of Easter

Risen Saviour,
    though we have not seen the empty tomb and folded grave-clothes,
    or the wounds in your hands and feet,
    yet we believe,
    for we have tasted your love,
    and, through your Holy Spirit,
    experienced the living reality of your presence,
    bringing joy, peace and fullness of life.
Deepen our faith in you as the Risen Lord.
Amen.

Third Sunday of Easter

Almighty God,
    we rejoice in the glorious fulfilment of your promises,
    the life, death and resurrection of your Son Jesus.
Open our hearts afresh to his presence in our lives,
    and to the new beginnings he daily makes possible
    through his gracious love.
Amen.

Fourth Sunday of Easter

Lord Jesus Christ,
 shepherd of the sheep,
 speak afresh of your great love –
 the way you seek us out,
 and willingly lay down your life for us,
 freely giving that we might freely receive.
Help us to follow you more closely,
 and trust you more completely.
Amen.

Fifth Sunday of Easter

Lord Jesus Christ,
 the true vine,
 help us to be strong and healthy branches.
May our lives be rooted in you,
 producing fruits of your Spirit –
 love, joy, peace and humility –
 that we may truly glorify your name,
 here and everywhere.
Amen.

Sixth Sunday of Easter

Living Lord Jesus,
 as we celebrate your resurrection,
 help us also to remember what made it possible:
 your readiness to endure the agony and anguish of the cross;
 your love so great that you were willing to lay down your life
 for our sake.
Write that truth once more in our hearts today,
 so that we may fulfil our mission to bear fruit that will last for ever.
Amen.

The Ascension of the Lord

Lord Jesus Christ,
   remind us through this day
   that you are king, but not of this world;
   that you rule, but not through force;
   that you invite our respect, but do not demand it;
   that you are the Lord of lords, but servant of all.
Give us a deeper understanding of your kingdom
   and a firmer grasp of your will.
Amen.

Seventh Sunday of Easter

Almighty and ever-living God,
   sanctify us in truth,
   so that we will love and serve you better.
Sanctify all we are and all we do,
   so that, consecrating our lives to your service,
   we may live each moment in the light of your love,
   your grace shining through our witness as light to the world,
   drawing together all people to you,
   through Jesus Christ our Lord.
Amen.

Pentecost

Spirit of God,
   fill us now as we praise you.
Sanctify our listening and thinking,
   our giving and doing,
   so that all we offer,
   and all we are,
   may reach *up* to you,
   and *out* to others,
   in joyful service.
  Amen.

Trinity Sunday

Eternal God,
  Father, Son and Holy Spirit,
  Lord of the past, the present and the future,
  with body, mind and spirit we worship you.
Open our eyes to your presence around us,
  our hearts to your love within us
  and our lives to your purpose beyond us.
Amen.

Second Sunday in Ordinary Time

Lord Jesus Christ,
  you know us better than we know ourselves,
  seeing us as we really are,
  with all our faults and weaknesses,
  yet graciously giving your all to set us free.
Help us to know *you* better in turn,
  so that, celebrating your awesome goodness,
  we may love you more deeply
  and follow you more faithfully,
  now and always.
Amen.

Third Sunday in Ordinary Time

Lord Jesus Christ,
  we celebrate the way you can take something ordinary
  and turn it into something special.
Take, then, our lives,
  and, by your Spirit, create us anew,
  that we may be your disciples,
  your body,
  your Church.
Amen.

Fourth Sunday in Ordinary Time

Lord Jesus Christ,
    as crowds in Galilee marvelled at your words and deeds,
    recognising in you an authority
    unlike anything they had seen before,
    speak your redeeming word to us in turn
    and reveal once more your renewing power.
Open our eyes to your saving grace and healing love,
    to all you are doing in our lives and our world today,
    so that the gospel might come alive for us each day.
Amen.

Fifth Sunday in Ordinary Time

Gracious God,
    may the good news of Jesus Christ kindle fresh faith within us.
Open our lives to the wonder of the gospel,
    so that, experiencing the joy and fulfilment it brings,
    we may share it with others.
Amen.

Sixth Sunday in Ordinary Time

Lord Jesus Christ,
    reach out through this time of prayer,
    and touch our lives with your healing power.
Speak your word of forgiveness and peace,
    and, through your Spirit, move within us
    and enfold us in your grace,
    that we may find true healing of body, mind and spirit.
Amen.

Seventh Sunday in Ordinary Time

Almighty God,
    we come before you,
    conscious of all that is wrong in our lives,
    yet knowing you are a God of love,
    slow to anger and swift to show mercy.
Through your Son, put your hand upon us,
    restore us
    and send us on our way to live and work for you.
Amen.

Eighth Sunday in Ordinary Time

Almighty God,
    as we come together in your presence
    save us from simply going through the motions of worship,
    doing what's expected of us.
Help us instead to see Jesus,
    and to recognise the way he is at work through his Spirit,
    both in our world and in our lives.
Meet with us,
    that we may walk each day with you.
Amen.

Ninth Sunday in Ordinary Time

Lord Jesus Christ,
    open our eyes today to a deeper awareness
    and yet more wonderful vision of who and what you are.
May your radiance burst afresh into our hearts,
    so that we may return to the daily routine of life
    determined there to know, love and serve you better,
    to the glory of your name.
Amen.

Tenth Sunday in Ordinary Time

God our Father,
 draw us together in faith and love
 with Christ and one another,
 to seek your kingdom and do your will.
Teach us what it means to be your children,
 your people,
 your family,
 and help us to honour you in all our dealings with each other.
Amen.

Eleventh Sunday in Ordinary Time

Loving God,
 by your grace plant new seeds of faith within us today,
 and through your Spirit feed and nurture them,
 so that they may grow and flourish within us.
Blossom in our lives,
 that we may sow seeds in the lives of others,
 for the growth of your kingdom.
Amen.

Twelfth Sunday in Ordinary Time

Lord Jesus Christ,
 fasten our thoughts on you
 and deepen our faith,
 so that, trusting you more completely,
 we will withstand the storms of trouble and tragedy,
 sickness and suffering.
Speak your word of peace,
 that we may find inner stillness and tranquillity of spirit,
 now and for evermore.
Amen.

Thirteenth Sunday in Ordinary Time

Almighty God,
give us a sense of your nearness as we worship you,
so that we may hear your voice
and learn more of your love in Christ.
Teach us, by the compassion he unfailingly showed
throughout his life and ministry,
to bring our broken lives and world before him,
opening all to his healing, restoring and life-giving touch.
Amen.

Fourteenth Sunday in Ordinary Time

Lord Jesus Christ,
keep us from being oblivious to your presence in our lives.
Open our lips to praise you,
our eyes to see you,
our ears to hear you
and our lives to serve you,
to the glory of your name.
Amen.

Fifteenth Sunday in Ordinary Time

Sovereign God,
open our hearts to everything you say to us
and send us out, in the power of your Spirit,
to be your disciples in the world.
Give us courage to speak your words,
and to live out our faith,
that others may hear the good news of Christ
and come to know you for themselves,
by his grace.
Amen.

Sixteenth Sunday in Ordinary Time

Living God,
   you know our needs better than we know them ourselves,
   you alone seeing into the heart
   and offering real peace.
So, then, we pray,
   work within us,
   draw us closer to you
   and increase our faith,
   so that we may find true fulfilment in your love,
   through Jesus Christ our Lord.
Amen.

Seventeenth Sunday in Ordinary Time

Lord Jesus Christ,
   as you used a little bread to feed the multitude,
   so use this time of worship to feed us.
Nourish us through your word,
   your Spirit
   and your grace,
   that our faith may be enriched
   and our commitment strengthened,
   such that you may use us in your service
   in ways beyond our expectations.
Amen.

Eighteenth Sunday in Ordinary Time

Living God,
   in a world that looks for instant satisfaction
   and fast food,
   we turn again to you,
   seeking lasting nourishment through Jesus Christ.
Come to us, we pray,
   and feed us once more,
   in body, mind and spirit.
Amen.

Nineteenth Sunday in Ordinary Time

Loving God,
    we cannot come to you except through Christ,
    the Bread of Life.
Help us to recognise his presence in the Eucharist
    and to respond with our whole heart and being.
Hear us and answer our prayer,
    by his grace.
Amen.

Twentieth Sunday in Ordinary Time

Lord Jesus Christ,
    the Bread of Life,
    giver of eternal joy and blessing,
    grant that through sharing in Mass today,
    we may draw closer to the Father
    and nearer to you,
    filled by your Spirit
    and sanctified by your grace.
Amen.

Twenty-first Sunday in Ordinary Time

Lord Jesus,
    we find your teaching hard to accept sometimes,
    more demanding than we feel comfortable with,
    yet we have found in you the message of eternal life.
Help us to believe that message,
    and, through experiencing your presence among us in the Eucharist,
    to find our faith deepened,
    our trust enriched
    and our love made stronger.
Amen.

Twenty-second Sunday in Ordinary Time

Almighty God,
  help us to celebrate Mass with heart and soul,
  with a true hunger and thirst to know and serve you better.
Work within us now,
  so that what we declare with our lips
  we may believe in our hearts and show in our lives,
  to your glory.
Amen.

Twenty-third Sunday in Ordinary Time

Lord,
  open our mouths to praise you,
  our ears to hear you
  and our hearts to love you.
Teach us that your grace,
  your word
  and your love
  are for everyone,
  your will being that all may marvel at your mighty acts
  and rejoice in your great goodness.
Amen.

Twenty-fourth Sunday in Ordinary Time

Lord Jesus Christ,
  we come to acknowledge you as Lord and Saviour,
  to profess our faith in you as the one who sets us free.
Give us courage to follow you,
  rejecting evil and willingly carrying the cross you give us,
  for the sake of the gospel.
Amen.

Twenty-fifth Sunday in Ordinary Time

Lord Jesus Christ,
   servant of all,
   teach us your way of gentleness and humility,
   so that we in turn may serve you and others.
Give us a childlike innocence and sincerity,
   trust and dependence,
   that we may be ready to grow in grace
   and respond in faith and love to your call.
Amen.

Twenty-sixth Sunday in Ordinary Time

Almighty God,
   we would draw close and learn of you,
   so that we may know, love and serve you better.
Give us a clearer understanding of your will
   and help us to recognise everything in our lives
   that leads us astray,
   separating us from you and one another.
Grant us grace to resist temptation,
   and to walk in your way,
   now and always.
Amen.

Twenty-seventh Sunday in Ordinary Time

Living God,
   in our relationships and friendships
   teach us to value and respect all people,
   recognising that everyone is precious to you,
   the work of your hands,
   made in your image.
Reach out now
   and put your Spirit within us,
   through Jesus Christ our Lord.
Amen.

Twenty-eighth Sunday in Ordinary Time

Almighty God,
   your word is unsettling,
   summoning us to service that seems beyond us.
Help us to hear your word and to make the changes it demands,
   for we know it offers the way to life;
   to peace, joy, hope and fulfilment,
   both now and for all eternity.
Amen.

Twenty-ninth Sunday in Ordinary Time

Almighty God,
   teach us to follow you not for *our* good but *yours*,
   seeking your glory and your kingdom.
Remind us that the way of Christ
   turns our understanding of life upside down,
   so that freedom is found in service,
   greatness in humility,
   strength in weakness,
   and eternal life through dying to self.
Help us to walk that way faithfully,
   in his strength and by his grace.
Amen.

Thirtieth Sunday in Ordinary Time

Lord Jesus Christ,
   as we gather to worship you,
   help us to see you here among us.
Give us a clearer picture of your greatness, power,
   love and mercy –
   a glimpse of you in all your glory,
   filling us with joy, faith, hope and love,
   now and always.
Amen.

Thirty-first Sunday in Ordinary Time

God our Father,
    we would love you with all our heart, understanding and strength,
    and would love our neighbour as ourselves,
    for in these we recognise the two greatest commandments,
    the fulfilment of the law.
Come, then, and put *your* love within us,
    so that it may shape all we offer and do.
Amen.

Thirty-second Sunday in Ordinary Time

Lord Jesus Christ,
    help us to hear again your call to discipleship,
    and faithfully to follow wherever you would lead.
May the good news of your living, dying and rising among us
    bring us to sincere repentance and deeper faith,
    so that we may live as your people,
    in the light of your kingdom.
Amen.

Thirty-third Sunday in Ordinary Time

Lord Jesus Christ,
    we look to you for wisdom and discernment,
    strength, support, guidance and inspiration.
Reveal to us your will,
    and help us to build your kingdom,
    confident that you will come again to reign here on earth,
    as you do already in heaven.
Amen.

Christ the King

Lord Jesus Christ,
    despised, rejected, yet risen and enthroned in glory,
    reign in our hearts and rule in our lives.
Grant that, as we sing your praises
    and acknowledge your greatness,
    we will follow your will in thought, word and deed,
    bringing honour always to you.
Amen.

YEAR C

First Sunday of Advent

Lord Jesus Christ,
   come among us in this season of Advent.
As you came in Bethlehem and will come again in glory,
   draw near now
   and open our eyes to your presence among us here.
Speak your word,
   grant your mercy
   and renew our faith,
   so that we may be ready at every moment to welcome you.
Amen.

Second Sunday of Advent

Lord Jesus Christ,
   prepare your way in our hearts
   and make us ready to worship you.
Renew our commitment
   and increase our love,
   so that we may be ready to follow you faithfully
   and serve you more generously.
Amen.

Third Sunday of Advent

Eternal God,
   we celebrate the fulfilment of your promises of old
   through the coming of the Messiah,
   foretold by the prophets and long yearned for.
We celebrate your honouring of those promises in Christ,
   granting through him more than we can ask or imagine.
Help us to celebrate your faithfulness
   and to trust you completely for the future,
   knowing that nothing can ever separate us from your love
   in Jesus Christ our Lord.
Amen.

Fourth Sunday of Advent

God our Father,
    just as Mary, when the angel had gone from her,
    went to care for her cousin,
    inspire us to serve each other with joy,
    opening our hearts in friendship,
    our homes in hospitality,
    and our lives in compassion.
Guide us to know and do your will,
    through Jesus Christ our Lord.
Amen.

Christmas Day

Eternal Father,
    as Mary and Joseph gazed on the Christ-child,
    so now we join with all your people across the centuries
    to welcome him into our lives
    true God yet true man,
    the Word made flesh,
    Jesus Christ our Lord.
As we celebrate his birth in the stable of Bethlehem,
    help us to know he is with us always,
    and to live each day in the light of that knowledge.
Amen.

The Holy Family

God our Father,
    as you drew Jesus even as a child to your house,
    calling him to seek you there and learn more of your will,
    so draw us to you in turn.
Through his words, deeds, life and ministry
    speak your word,
    and through his living presence renew your love in us
    and help us to follow your will.
Amen.

Second Sunday of Christmas

Lord Jesus Christ,
 come among us through your Spirit,
 and grant us grace upon grace.
Open our hearts to you,
 and help us to welcome you as the Word made flesh,
 the Light of the World,
 the source and giver of life.
Amen.

The Epiphany of the Lord

Lord Jesus Christ,
 Light of the World,
 shine in our hearts,
 banishing all that obscures your goodness
 and darkens our lives.
Come to us
 and flood our lives with the radiance of your love,
 so that it may shine *in* us
 and *through* us –
 for all people to see.
Amen.

The Baptism of the Lord

Almighty God,
 challenge us through the example of Jesus
 and his humble acceptance of baptism from John in the Jordan.
As you affirmed him as your beloved Son,
 the one on whom your favour rests,
 help us to know that you affirm us also
 as your children,
 loved and cherished,
 chosen and precious in your sight.
Amen.

Ash Wednesday

God our Father,
    through this season of Lent
    deepen our faith
    and draw us closer to you,
    that we may receive pardon and cleansing,
    and find strength to walk more faithfully in the days ahead,
    through Jesus Christ our Lord.
Amen.

First Sunday of Lent

Living God,
    we are easily led astray,
    lured from what really matters by the things of this world,
    enticed into compromising our commitment
    and flouting your will.
During this season of Lent
    call us back to you,
    so that when temptation comes
    we will stay as true to you as you are to us.
Amen.

Second Sunday of Lent

Almighty God,
    just as in the transfigured Christ
    you offered a glimpse of your radiance,
    so may we today see your glory more clearly –
    your light shining in our hearts,
    and filling us with joy.
Keep us always open to new horizons,
    new insights,
    aware that, however much we know of you,
    you have far more to reveal,
    more than we can yet understand.
Amen.

Third Sunday of Lent

Loving God,
  we are conscious of our repeated disobedience to your will,
  our inability to serve as you would like.
Help us to be truly penitent,
  confident that your love and mercy endures for ever.
Strengthen our faith during this season
  so that our lives may fully bear fruit in your service.
Amen.

Fourth Sunday of Lent

Lord Jesus,
  though we have often forgotten you and gone our own way,
  squandering your blessing and ignoring your guidance,
  still you long to welcome us back,
  your arms outstretched to embrace us once more.
Help us to seek forgiveness
  through confession, penance and reconciliation,
  that our hearts may always be open to receive your love and mercy.
Amen.

Fifth Sunday of Lent

Lord Jesus Christ,
  just as you showed love and compassion
  to the woman caught in adultery,
  refusing to condemn
  but offering instead forgiveness and healing,
  the opportunity to start afresh with the slate wiped clean,
  so, we ask, fill us with love in our dealings with others,
  and help us to know your healing and forgiveness for ourselves.
Amen.

Palm Sunday

Lord Jesus Christ,
   teach us today not just to welcome you as king,
   but also to commit ourselves to your kingdom,
   putting our lives at your disposal for you to use as you will.
Take our faith, witness and service;
   our gifts, time and money;
   our thoughts, words and deeds;
   and use all to fulfil your royal purpose,
   to your glory.
Amen.

Maundy Thursday

Lord Jesus Christ,
   remind us today that you were broken for *us* –
   that you endured the agony of the cross to set us free
   and the darkness of death to bring us life,
   but remind us also that your purpose embraces *all*,
   in every place and time.
Speak throughout this holy season of all you have done
   and seek yet to do,
   and help us, by your grace, to reach out to others in turn,
   with your love,
   in your name.
Amen.

Good Friday

Lord Jesus Christ,
   though we can never repay the price you paid to redeem us,
   we want to acknowledge your goodness,
   to express our gratitude for your awesome love
   and immense sacrifice.
Receive, then, our worship and thanks,
   the faith we declare and the discipleship we offer,
   for we bring all humbly to you,
   with body, mind and soul.
Amen.

Easter Day

Renewing and life-giving God,
    as we celebrate again your victory over death
    and triumph over evil,
    open our hearts today to the way you are able to change our lives
    and transform our world.
Remind us of your resurrection power all around us,
    bringing hope out of despair,
    joy out of sorrow,
    peace out of turmoil
    and love out of hatred,
    and in that faith may we live now and trust for the future,
    assured that nothing can defeat your purpose
    or deny the life you offer for all eternity,
    through Jesus Christ our Lord.
Amen.

Second Sunday of Easter

Risen Christ,
    meet with us afresh today,
    so that the worship we share in may be *our* worship,
    the faith we proclaim be *our* faith
    and the joy we celebrate be *our* joy.
Come among us through your Spirit
    and lead us to deeper knowledge of the truth,
    so that the good news will bring forth fruit in loving service
    and joyful witness,
    to the glory of your name.
Amen.

Third Sunday of Easter

Risen Lord,
  recalling the love and mercy you showed to Peter,
  the way you so graciously restored him,
  commissioning him to be shepherd of your flock,
  so we pray for those today entrusted with pastoral oversight:
  parish clergy, bishops, cardinals and pope,
  all who bear the privilege yet responsibility of ministry.
May they be true shepherds of your flock in our time,
  to your glory.
Amen.

Fourth Sunday of Easter

Lord Jesus Christ,
  just as your words and actions were one –
  each reinforcing the other so that everything you said and did
  testified to the loving purpose of your Father in heaven –
  so may our lives likewise speak with one voice,
  bearing eloquent witness
  to your transforming power and redeeming love,
  and to the joy, hope, peace and purpose we have found in you.
Speak to us now,
  so that everything we are may speak for you always,
  to the glory of your name.
Amen.

Fifth Sunday of Easter

Lord Jesus Christ,
  we come to you in prayer,
  seeking to learn more of you
  and to welcome you more fully into our lives.
Help us to love as you have loved us,
  so that others will know we are your disciples.
Help us, during this Mass,
  to recognise the ways in which we fall short of that calling,
  and to open our hearts afresh to your grace,
  so that your love may grow within us
  and overflow to your praise and glory.
Amen.

Sixth Sunday of Easter

All-powerful God,
   come among us through your Holy Spirit,
   so that we may know and do your holy will.
Grant us an inner experience of your presence,
   unfolding your word,
   granting your peace
   and nurturing your love within us.
   So may we honour you not just here and now,
   but in every place and at all times,
   through keeping your commands and living as your people.
Amen.

The Ascension of the Lord

Saviour Christ,
   King of kings and Lord of lords,
   we offer you our praise and adoration,
   expressing our love and gratitude for all you have done,
   and offering our lives back to you in joyful response.
Come among us now, through your Spirit,
   and reveal your glory.
Fill us afresh with your grace,
   and help us truly to bless your holy name.
Amen.

Seventh Sunday of Easter

Gracious God,
   open our hearts afresh today to fullness of life –
   life lived in union with you,
   in harmony with your will
   and in the light of your love.
Draw us closer to your side,
   and overcome whatever separates us from you
   or from each other –
   everything that undermines the unity you want us to share –
   so that the world may believe in Jesus whom you have sent.
Amen.

Pentecost

Holy Spirit,
   speak to us through the Scriptures,
   through prayer and sacrament
   and through each other.
May your fruits grow within us,
   your gifts be freely given,
   your power displayed
   and your counsel given.
Open our hearts to all you would say
   and all you would do among us,
   through Jesus Christ our Lord.
Amen.

Trinity Sunday

Most blessed Trinity,
   mighty and mysterious,
   before all,
   within all,
   above all,
   we praise you in all your wonder and holiness.
Give us today a fuller sense of your greatness,
   a deeper awareness of your presence
   and a firmer understanding of your will,
   that we may worship, love and serve you
   in spirit and in truth,
   through Jesus Christ our Lord.
Amen.

Second Sunday in Ordinary Time

Lord Jesus Christ,
   come among us and, by your grace,
   work your miracle of renewal once more in our hearts.
As you transformed water into wine at Cana,
   bless us too with your grace,
   so that where joy is lacking and hope exhausted,
   the new wine of your presence will bring us rekindled faith,
   our lives revitalised through your love.
Amen.

Third Sunday in Ordinary Time

Lord Jesus Christ,
    as you expounded the Scriptures during your earthly ministry,
    unfolding their true meaning,
    unfold them to us now,
    through your Spirit.
Open our minds and hearts to all you say to us,
    that we may grasp more clearly the nature of your kingdom
    and the response you call us to make.
Amen.

Fourth Sunday in Ordinary Time

God our Father,
    speak through the Apostle Paul of your great gift of love:
    the love you hold for us
    and that you call us to show to others in turn.
Help us to recognise that without love we are nothing,
    and so may we put that at the centre of all we do,
    through the grace of Jesus Christ our Lord.
Amen.

Fifth Sunday in Ordinary Time

Lord Jesus Christ,
    we remember how your first disciples left everything to follow you,
    responding wholeheartedly to your call.
We recognise your call to faith and discipleship in turn,
    to being your witnesses in our time.
Help us to respond generously,
    that we may speak your word
    and embody your love in our world,
    to the glory of your name.
Amen.

Sixth Sunday in Ordinary Time

Lord Jesus Christ,
  help us to worship you in spirit and truth
  by truly living as your people,
  walking in your way and honouring your will.
Help us to understand what it means
  to be part of your kingdom here on earth,
  and so may we find in you our lasting joy.
Amen.

Seventh Sunday in Ordinary Time

Lord Jesus Christ,
  we come to you,
  remembering that you did not simply talk about love,
  but showed it, even on the cross,
  forgiving those who persecuted you and showing compassion to all.
Receive our love today,
  and, by your grace, increase it,
  so that it may reach out to all –
  friends, enemies and neighbours.
Amen.

Eighth Sunday in Ordinary Time

Lord Jesus Christ,
  help us to see the good in others before the bad,
  responding generously and with open hearts to those we meet.
Help us to recognise the bad in ourselves as well as the good,
  the faults as much as the virtues,
  and give us courage to change where we need to,
  so that our lives may produce good fruit for you.
Amen.

Ninth Sunday in Ordinary Time

Lord Jesus Christ,
   through everything you have accomplished in so many lives,
   responding to people's cry for help
   and ministering to their needs,
   inspire us and increase our faith.
Encourage us through the faith of others:
   their trust in your power and purpose,
   their willingness to follow where you lead,
   their confidence in your unfailing love.
Enthrall us through the way the good news continues to change lives,
   capturing the hearts of individuals the world over.
Speak to us now,
   so that we may trust you more,
   love you better
   and serve you more effectively,
   to the glory of your name.
Amen.

Tenth Sunday in Ordinary Time

Almighty God,
   remind us today of your power, strength and authority,
   your ability to create out of nothing
   and to re-create through the word of Christ.
Teach us that nothing is beyond you;
   that you are constantly fashioning our lives,
   day after day bringing new beginnings and fresh hope;
   new life even out of death.
Help us, then, whatever we face,
   and however inadequate our resources may seem
   to meet life's challenges,
   to put our faith in you,
   knowing that you will hear and answer.
Amen.

Eleventh Sunday in Ordinary Time

Lord Jesus Christ,
   help us today to recognise the depth of your love
   and the extent of your mercy,
   and to respond gladly,
   offering you heartfelt praise
   and a life consecrated in every part to your service.
May we honour you through the people we are
   and the lives we live,
   your love flowing within us always,
   and spilling over in generous and joyful response to you and others,
   to the glory of your name.
Amen.

Twelfth Sunday in Ordinary Time

Almighty God,
   in all the trials and traumas of life,
   and in our troubled world,
   remind us that you are with us in good times and bad,
   sharing in our sorrow and suffering,
   understanding our fear and anxiety,
   and seeking to strengthen and heal us.
Teach us during this Mass that though life may test us to the limit,
   nothing can ever separate us from your love,
   poured out through Jesus Christ our Lord.
Amen.

Thirteenth Sunday in Ordinary Time

Lord Jesus Christ,
   teach us today to put you first in our lives,
   seeking to honour and serve you wholeheartedly,
   truly committed in body, mind and spirit.
May our response to you shape everything we do
   and all we are,
   so that, by your grace, we will faithfully walk your way
   and live to your glory.
Amen.

Fourteenth Sunday in Ordinary Time

Living God,
   through our being at Mass today,
   equip us to go out in your name,
   returning to our homes, families and friends,
   our places of work and leisure,
   and showing there,
   through word and deed,
   our faith in Christ.
Fill us with the courage we need to answer your call,
   that through our discipleship and witness
   you may bring closer your kingdom,
   through Jesus Christ our Lord.
Amen.

Fifteenth Sunday in Ordinary Time

Living God,
   help us to understand more clearly today
   that loving you must show itself in loving others;
   that commitment should spill over into compassion,
   faith into works
   and prayer into service.
Like the Good Samaritan of your parable,
   open our eyes to the needs of our neighbours,
   both near and far,
   and help us wherever possible
   to express something of your care and concern for all,
   ministering to them in the name of Christ.
Amen.

Sixteenth Sunday in Ordinary Time

Almighty and eternal God,
  help us, as we gather here once more,
  truly to focus on you;
  to listen again to your word
  and hear what you say to us,
  so that we may return to the daily routine,
  strengthened and encouraged,
  with deeper insight and a fresh perspective,
  through Jesus Christ our Lord.
Amen.

Seventeenth Sunday in Ordinary Time

Almighty God,
  help us to grasp more clearly today that you call us your children
  and want us to relate to you as our Father;
  that you value every one of us,
  taking pleasure in our presence
  and delighting to give us good things.
Teach us to live in the light of that truth,
  turning to you each day
  for the guidance and blessing you so freely offer,
  and seeking above all the indwelling of your Spirit,
  through which *you* live in *us*
  and *we* in *you*.
Amen.

Eighteenth Sunday in Ordinary Time

Loving God,
    remind us again today of the nature of your kingdom,
    and help us to live accordingly.
Teach us that the treasures you give,
    whether earthly or heavenly,
    are not to be hoarded but shared,
    consecrated back to you in your service
    for the benefit of others.
Grant us, then, generosity of spirit,
    so that we will understand the true meaning of riches
    and be ready to give as freely as we have received,
    through Jesus Christ our Lord.
Amen.

Nineteenth Sunday in Ordinary Time

Eternal God,
    teach us to use the time, gifts,
    health and opportunities you give us,
    wisely,
    creatively
    and fruitfully.
Remind us here once more today of what you ask of us –
    the responsibilities involved in Christian discipleship –
    and, by your grace,
    help us not to be found wanting.
Amen.

Twentieth Sunday in Ordinary Time

Living God,
   reveal to us more of your will,
   and give us wisdom and courage to follow it.
Save us from taking the path of least resistance,
   opting for peace where there is no peace
   or pretending all is well when it is not.
Give us instead the faith and courage we need
   to stand up for what is right,
   even if that risks alienating people,
   including, perhaps, those we love.
Hear us and help us, O God,
   in the name of Christ.
Amen.

Twenty-first Sunday in Ordinary Time

Gracious God,
   teach us to recognise that neither religion nor worship
   are an end in themselves,
   but that each is designed to lead us closer to you
   that we might work more effectively for your kingdom
   here on earth.
Help us to avoid reducing faith to rules and regulations,
   outward show rather than inner experience.
Through this Mass kindle true faith within us,
   by the grace of Jesus Christ our Lord.
Amen.

Twenty-second Sunday in Ordinary Time

Almighty God,
  teach us to love without demanding we are loved first,
  to serve without expecting service,
  to give without seeking gifts,
  to show compassion to others even when none is returned.
Remind us, as we celebrate Mass,
  that you have shown just such love in Christ,
  just such service, generosity and compassion,
  and, by your grace, grant that something of you
  may shine through us,
  to the glory of your name.
Amen.

Twenty-third Sunday in Ordinary Time

Eternal Father,
  help us today to grasp more clearly
  that it is in giving we receive,
  in losing we find,
  in sacrifice we find reward,
  and in dying to self that we rise to new life.
In that knowledge, may we willingly accept the cost of discipleship,
  knowing that whatever is asked of us,
  the rewards of your kingdom are beyond price.
Open our eyes afresh today to that truth,
  through Jesus Christ our Lord.
Amen.

Twenty-fourth Sunday in Ordinary Time

Lord Jesus Christ,
    we thank you that, however often we go astray,
    you love us enough to seek us out,
    always ready to welcome us back as your children.
So we come to Mass,
    called by your love,
    knowing that though, like lost sheep,
    we have wandered from your side
    and gone our own way,
    you welcome us joyfully
    and without reserve.
Amen.

Twenty-fifth Sunday in Ordinary Time

Living God,
    speak to us again of the things in life that really matter,
    that offer true joy and lasting fulfilment,
    for we so easily forget.
Remind us that the riches of this world can sometimes rule us,
    and teach us instead to use them wisely and generously,
    setting our hearts above all on treasures in heaven –
    the blessings of joy, hope, love and peace,
    life in abundance that you alone offer.
Open our lives now to receive and respond,
    through Jesus Christ our Lord.
Amen.

Twenty-sixth Sunday in Ordinary Time

Almighty Father,
    teach us never to forget those who have less:
    the hungry and homeless,
    the poor and underprivileged,
    those denied the healthcare, education
    and other resources we take for granted.
Remind us that in serving the poor we serve you,
    contributing in some way, however small,
    to the growth of your kingdom.
Amen.

Twenty-seventh Sunday in Ordinary Time

Lord of all,
    remind us today that you are a faithful and loving God,
    a God who hears the cry of your people
    and answers them in their distress.
Though you do not guarantee freedom from pain, sorrow or hardship,
    you promise always, through the inner presence of your Spirit,
    to give us strength to meet adversity,
    peace even in turmoil
    and laughter even through tears.
Help us to trust you whatever life brings,
    through Jesus Christ our Lord.
Amen.

Twenty-eighth Sunday in Ordinary Time

Almighty and ever-living God,
    speak to us afresh through your word during Mass.
As Jesus healed the sick
    and responded to the cry of the needy,
    continue to reach out today.
Teach us that, through your great love and power,
    you are able to turn sorrow to joy
    and darkness to light –
    bringing good out of evil –
    and fill us with thanksgiving for the ways,
    in our own lives,
    we have found that to be true.
Amen.

Twenty-ninth Sunday in Ordinary Time

God our loving Father,
   we bring you our prayers,
    knowing that you are always ready to hear and answer.
Remind us once more of that truth today,
   and help us to believe it in our hearts,
   so that we may pray each day,
   entrusting ourselves to you
   and leaving all safely in your hands,
   through Jesus Christ our Lord.
Amen.

Thirtieth Sunday in Ordinary Time

Gracious God,
   we come to you in prayer,
   knowing that you are close to the broken-hearted
   and hear the cry of the poor in spirit.
Hear *our* cry,
   and put a new heart and right spirit within us.
   for we know our sins and yearn for forgiveness.
Renew us, we pray,
   for we cannot do it ourselves.
Receive, accept and use us by your grace,
   for your kingdom's sake.
Amen.

Thirty-first Sunday in Ordinary Time

Lord Jesus Christ,
   like Zacchaeus, give us today true eagerness and determination
   to see and hear you for ourselves.
Give us honesty and humility when we hear your call
   to admit our faults and be truly sorry;
   to welcome you into our lives
   and do what we can to make amends.
Help us to show our gratitude for all you have done
   by striving to offer faithful service in return,
   through Jesus Christ our Lord.
Amen.

Thirty-second Sunday in Ordinary Time

Almighty God,
   refresh our faith as we celebrate Mass,
   rekindling our trust in your eternal will
   and our confidence that nothing can separate us from your love.
In that assurance we remember once more the faithful departed,
   asking that you will receive them into your kingdom
   and give them your peace.
Amen.

Thirty-third Sunday in Ordinary Time

Living God,
   teach us to trust in your future
   and to keep faith in the final fulfilment of your kingdom.
Despite every temptation to turn away,
   help us to serve and honour you
   through following the way of Christ,
   consecrating each moment to you,
   and leaving all else in your hands.
Amen.

Christ the King

Lord Jesus Christ,
   we celebrate you as King,
   crowned with thorns yet also with glory,
   lifted up on a cross yet exalted on high,
   laid in a tomb yet honoured as the risen Lord.
Teach us through our Mass that,
   just as you brought joy out of sorrow,
   hope out of despair
   and life out of death,
   so you still change lives today,
   bringing light into our darkness
   and healing in our brokenness.
Reach out in love
   and lead us into your kingdom.
Amen.

SPECIAL FEAST DAYS

Mary, Mother of God – 1 January

Loving God,
    speak to us today through the faith of Mary:
    her humility, trust and obedience,
    her willingness to be used as you saw fit
    and to accept that what is beyond human power
    is nevertheless possible for you.
May the grace she embodied fill us in turn,
    through her Son, our Saviour,
    Jesus Christ our Lord.
Amen.

The Presentation of the Lord (Candlemas) – 2 February

Lord Jesus Christ,
    remembering how, at the time for purification,
    Mary brought you to the temple,
    and how Simeon greeted you there as a light to the nations,
    so we come today,
    asking that you will purify our hearts,
    fill us with light,
    and make us new,
    revealing your great love *to* and *through* us,
    to the glory of your name.
Amen.

St John the Baptist – 24 June

Lord Jesus Christ,
    for the way John the Baptist prepared the way for your coming,
    pointing to you through word and deed,
    and speaking the truth despite the cost,
    we praise you.
Inspire us through his example,
    that we may be more ready to serve you
    and, through our life and witness,
    to prepare your way in turn
    in the hearts and minds of those around us.
Amen.

St Peter and St Paul – 29 June

Living God,
    as you called Peter and Paul to proclaim the gospel
    and build up your Church,
    so help us to hear and respond in turn,
    living faithfully as your people
    and testifying to the good news of Christ.
Amen.

The Transfiguration of the Lord – 6 August

Lord Jesus Christ,
    as Peter, James and John witnessed your glory on the mountaintop,
    so, through your word,
    our fellowship
    and the experience of your living presence,
    may we glimpse your greatness more fully
    and know you more completely.
Amen.

The Assumption – 15 August

Lviing God,
    speak through the faith, commitment,
    trust and obedience of Mary,
    which you so graciously and gloriously honoured,
    and instil in us the same virtues and qualities,
    the same love and humility,
    so that, in the fullness of time,
    we may share with her in the same kingdom.
Amen.

The Triumph of the Holy Cross – 14 September

Lord Jesus Christ,
  speak through the holy cross of your great goodness –
  your readiness to suffer and die
  to bring life in all its fullness to our world.
Speak of humility and victory,
  grace and hope,
  love and mercy,
  endings and new beginnings –
  of the gift you won there for all:
  life as God's children.
Amen.

All Saints' Day – 1 November

God of history,
  we thank you for your faithfulness in every age,
  the guidance and love you have unfailingly shown.
We praise you for saints of every race and culture,
  men and women who show us the way to holiness.
Speak to us through them,
  that we may speak to others of you,
  through Jesus Christ our Lord.
Amen.

Feasts of the Dedication of a Church

Loving God,
  for bringing this church into being
  and nurturing your people here across the years,
  we praise you.
As we dedicate ourselves and this place once more to you,
  remembering the past and anticipating the future,
  speak of your faithfulness,
  your presence
  and your promise to be with us always,
  and in that light may we live faithfully, to your glory,
  through Jesus Christ our Lord.
Amen.